Heroic Measures

Books by David Bergman

Poetry

Cracking the Code (1985)
The Care and Treatment of Pain (1994)

Criticism

Gaiety Transfigured: Gay Self-Representation in American
  Literature (1991)

Edited Collections

The Violet Quill Reader: The Emergence of Gay Writing
  after Stonewall (1994)
Strategic Camp: Style and Homosexuality (1994)
Men on Men 5: Best New Gay Fiction (1994)
Men on Men 6: Best New Gay Fiction (1996)

Heroic Measures

David Bergman

Ohio State University Press
Columbus

Library of Congress Cataloging-in-Publication Data

Bergman, David, 1950–
    Heroic measures / David Bergman.
        p. cm.
        ISBN 0-8142-0783-9 (alk. paper). — ISBN 0-8142-0784-7 (pbk. :
    alk. paper)
    1. Gay men—poetry. I. Title.
    PS3552.E71933H4 1998
    811' .54—dc21   97–52322
                                                CIP

Type set in Adobe Bembo.
Printed by Braun-Brumfield, Inc.

9 8 7 6 5 4 3 2 1

Acknowledgements

The American Scholar: "My Father Almost Ascending," "A Father's Blessing," and "A Dream of Nightingales"
Appalachia: "In the Summer Crucible"
Art & Understanding: "The Care and Treatment of Pain," "The Witness to the Arrest," and "Days of the 1970s."
The Baltimore Alternative: "A House of Two Women"
The Kenyon Review: "Heroic Measures" and "A World of Difference"
Mid-American Review: "The Great Trans-Atlantic Hot-Air Balloon Race" and "Mapplethorpe's Lily"
Nebo: An earlier version of "Pictures at an Eakins Exhibition"
The New Criterion: "Daughters Denying the Dreams of Their Fathers"
The New Republic: "Death and the Young Man" and "Goya's Enlightenment"
The Paris Review: "The Guide of Tiresias" and "Benny"
Poetry: "In the Waiting Room" and "Bonzai for Beginners"
Raritan: "Primal Scene" and "A Part for Horn"
The Western Humanities Review: "Along Hadrian's Wall"

"Mapplethorpe's Lily" appeared in *The 1995 Anthology of Magazine Verse* (Monitor Books).

"The Care and Treatment of Pain" appeared in *Things Shaped in Passing* (Persea).

"In the Waiting Room" has been reprinted in *Sutured Words: Contemporary Poetry about Medicine* (Aviva Press), and with "A Dream of Nightingales" in *Poets for Life: Seventy-Six Poets Respond to AIDS* (Crown). "A Dream of Nightingales" was set to music by Ned Rorem and performed in Alice Tully Hall as part of the *AIDS Quilt Song Book* and has been reprinted in *The Name of Love: Classic Gay Love Poems* (St. Martin's).

Many of the poems appeared in the chapbook *The Care and Treatment of Pain* (Kairos Editions).

for
Daniel Mark Epstein

Contents

I

Death and the Young Man

(after Schubert)

"Death, you needn't be afraid,
thin and fevered though I am.
I, who have waited so long
to see you, will not struggle
now that you've arrived. Just be
gentle. This is my first time."

"Yes, I was frightened. Though I
have taken many ravaged
by Time and Cruelty, yet
not until now, one like you
so beautiful and ready.
Let me hold you in my arms."

Benny

Ellen and I go back, way back, at least as far
as her pre-op days when she was still a man
and minced each midnight through the local bar.

Now that she's a woman everything's changed.
She's faithful to her Unisex salon, gets in
on time to make sure everything's arranged

and when she's out, she never touches gin.
I stop by every couple of weeks to chat
and keep the top from showing where it's thin.

She's glad to oblige: so few are left and not
one who remembers Benny, a legendary
hunk in his day—those days when men were hot.

Unlike your classic beauty, Benny was hairy—
the sweaty curls mapped out his musculature,
his torso was split by a dark and furry

line that took wing beneath his pectorals
in the shower at the gym, his legs were streaked
like marble, his ass circled with bristling whorls—

he was Miss Five O'clock Shadow from the neck
down! It's almost a decade Benny's been gone
but I can see him now cruising the meatrack

with his skin so pale it seemed made of bone,
and his "curvaceous" calves crammed into fishnet
stockings. We used to watch him stand alone,

in hot pants, cowboy boots and a baby bonnet
tied beneath his chin with a bright pink bow,
twirling a parasol with gold fringe on it

while the cars on Eager Street drove by real slow
then raced away as he waved his white-gloved hand.
Ellen and I agree he was lucky to go

with his looks intact, quick, an accident—
falling drunk, they say, down a flight of stairs,
or maybe several flights, from his top-floor flat.

at least it's better than how others fare,
all the boys since Benny who've come to work
in Ellen's shop, at Ellen's other chair.

Old Voices at a New Number

My voice alone? Or are there others
he telephones who are willing to repeat
his fantasies to him, play the pond to his
    overbearing Narcissus?

Every month or so he'd ring me up
without regard to time of day. When I moved
he slipped my mind. But there he was this morning:
    old voice at a new number.

His conversations still start the same:
He tells me he's been thinking of me and now
stark naked either lies in his bed or stands
    dripping from his hot shower,

asking, "What are you up to?" my cue
to begin a mantra of desire which lasts
until the line goes dead, when he rests the limp
    receiver like an infant

back into its awaiting cradle.
All the while his speech is reduced to gurgles
of muted arousal and then the sharp, quick gasps
    of semantic release.

On previous calls, I've tried to change
the scenario—supply new positions,
players, plots—as though these images as old
    as the earth, if not older

(for he who fathered Time must
have entertained some idle moments) needed
constant innovation, novelty
    to spark the passing fancy.

But he'd always draw me back
to the few choice words proven to excite him,
phrases that held a strange abiding power
    of free association.

I could sense them easing
the cork from his bottled up feelings and burst
spontaneous overflows of emotion.
    Ask me why I continued

to speak what had long since failed
to incite my passion's dimmest flickering,
risk that his wife (newly wed) might uncover
    our alien affection

and confuse our star-crossed wires
for a more intimate connection, name me
as corespondent on a bill of divorce,
    I can muster no defense

but that pleasure delayed is pleasure
denied, and who would deny him that pleasure,
to hear the mystery of Flesh made Word,
    the carnal incarnation?

What harm can be in knowing such joy?
I think of him before his ledgers, adding
the long columns of his soundless auditing
    where figures of speech are banned

and only those numbers that balance
are allowed a place in his unspeakable
accounts. Would some purer language ever bring
      an approximate comfort?

    Could he appreciate a different
music than the one of our vernacular?
Or is our low dialect, this underground
      argot dug from the bowels

    of the dark heart, this precious metal
unexpurgated and unrefined, this thick
inflected foreign tongue, as close as we will
      ever come to poetry?

The Window

All that spring I was afraid to stand
near windows for fear I'd throw myself
out of one. Twice I had found myself
flung from a chair and making a run
for it, driven by dreams of leaping
clear of the pain of his desertion:
my lover of five years who one day
in midwinter needed more distance
from a life he felt had grown too close.

Then one morning a cat was howling
in the courtyard of my building. There
he sat, a miniature tiger
in the shade of the Japanese plum.
He showed passersby his needlelike
incisors and his bright coral tongue,
but if given a minute, he'd come
to press his flanks against your ankle,
then flip round to have his belly rubbed.

It took me no time to discover
he was defenseless as a kitten—
stripped of balls and claws, a Chippendale
sofa cut down to Shaker size. I
brought him food and water, then waited
for his owners to arrive for him.
Surely they knew he'd never survive,
denatured as he was, through the wild
predatory darkness of late May.

But at midnight he was still down there,
batting the moths at the lamppost and
ringing the ivory carillon
hung in the lilies-of-the-valley.
What else could I do but bring him up
to my fourth floor apartment? I slashed
the latest pages of the *Times,* then
filled a Macy's box with the litter,
placed box and cat on my screened-in porch,
closed the stiff French doors and went to bed.

Next morning he was gone. I could see
the corner where he butted his head
until the screen gave way and the leaf
that he left on the ledge, curled and brown
like a mouse, a gift for my concern.
I couldn't bear to look. I turned and ran
four flights down to where I'd knew he'd land—
a bank of ivy—and found—nothing—
not a dent in the thick ground cover.

The Wrath of Medea

I know Medea's anger but can't quote
the lines she speaks, when hands about the throat
of her child, she feels his pulse beneath her thumb.
I know because I've felt that numb.

And I have smelt the stench of sweet revenge
rise up like a drunkard on a binge
to swat the snakes that coil about his brain.
Hieronymo's mad againe.

And then there comes the buzzing of the flies
swarming like pupils severed from their eyes,
roaring in the ears of pale Orestes.
I, too, have had my share of Furies

and felt the double-edge of your betrayal
perforate my heart as though in Braille
you wrote so in my blindness I could see:
By your love I was imprisoned, by your pain set free.

In the Waiting Room

St. Gaudens would have known what would suit
this research institution: a tall,
stately figure of Science, proudly
undeterred, her plain draperies hung
in even rows to soften the cast
of her bronze body, one hand aloft
raising a hypodermic needle.

Before such images, these six-month
checkups would seem like pilgrimages
in which unpardonable clerics
and unbathed wives had walked before us.
But in this vast, unadorned building
guided by efficiency alone
there's no distraction from my purpose.

With only the pages of *People*
and *Time* for amusement, who would not
feel afraid? For I am here as part
of a study on the life cycle
of the adult homosexual,
to see which of us will sicken next
in our group of twelve hundred odd

from this strange disease of yet unknown
beginnings that teaches the body
how to betray the life within it.
An endangered species, we are watched
to see how it makes its first appearance
and all the stages on which it acts
in our theatre of operations.

Sometimes two or three men are waiting
to be called—not by name—but number
to preserve our anonymity
(although who in the face of such cool
clinical detachment could retain
a sense of self?). Yet at times one might
see a friend or distant acquaintance

head down or looking to the wall
(there are no windows here) marking where
the plaster has given way. I stop,
exchange a few meaningless phrases
and perhaps he'll have a joke to tell
or news of someone known in common
until the silence descends once more.

But once, early for my appointment,
I was left alone when voices shot
through the swinging doors. A man in a white
laboratory coat and another
clad in jeans were speaking, and I knew
that the man in denim had become
the person I feared that I might be.

And I hated him for having brought
his death so near that I could touch it,
and the room seemed to fill with the dread
odor of his dying, and I sat amazed:
for with his neat beard and curly hair
and the whiteness of his freckled face,
he might be taken for my lover.

Now the two were arguing in that
complicitous tone of handymen
faced with a machine that will not work.
What about this? Or that? they question,
uncertain which, if any, repairs
to undertake, running their cold hands
along his ailing anatomy.

"I'll never live through that," the patient
laughs, as though it were another's case
they were discussing. I asked myself,
can this be true? Can people withdraw
so far from their existence that life
and death become academic games
left to pique their curiosity,

a trivial pursuit that will not
bore when played for hours at a time?
Or is there some catharsis unknown
to me, when what you fear will happen
happens and there's nothing more to fear,
and one reaches that calm meadow where
the sacred few are allowed to rest

beyond the walled, polluted city
that cast them out? They are gone away
now out of sight through another set
of fire doors, but I can still hear
their faint comforting voices whisper
in the hushed tones of lovers careful
not to wake the disapproving crowd.

A nurse approaches, clipboard in hand.
Have I brought my paraphernalia,
samples of semen and excrement
which the study cannot do without?
And the old terror revives in me
of what they will find: the truth, perhaps,
that I like everyone else will die.

Bring him back, bring him back, the one who
gave me his healing touch. I'm ready
to embrace him now if he can stop
the pain of losing what was never
mine to keep. Bring him back
so he can teach me how to be
content when I take his place at last.

Days of the 1970s

The memory rises up and fades
when my youthful lover asks to know
what love was like before there was AIDS.

I could tell him about my escapades
on planes, in trains, aboard the Metro.
But the memory rises up and fades.

What of bath-house tricks? And tea room trades
with a living Michelangelo?
(Oh, how we loved before there was AIDS!)

Our militant joys marched in parades
that stretched in a line from the Pines to the Castro
as the memory rises up and fades.

Trucks and parks. Vice squad raids.
Underaged boys dressed in drag for a show
whom we showered with love before they got AIDS.

In sweaters, feathers, chains and brocades,
we danced till the dawn crept sticky and slow
like a memory that conveniently fades
on what love was like before there was AIDS.

The Care and Treatment of Pain

in memory of Allen Barnett

I came to learn what the well can learn
from the dying and the gravely sick:
the fine art of living with the quick
unknitting of flesh. Tired and gaunt,
he faced me across the small banquette
and spoke as rare and welcomed rains
steamed up, like smoke from a cigarette,
the dark windows of the restaurant.

"See these bubbles rising from my head,
purple cancers 'winking at the brim'
which nothing's stopped, not even a grim
experiment with interferon
shot straight into my tumorous scalp.
So far the only result has been
I can find how far the lesions spread
by counting the needles going in.

Yet by the eighth I seem to lose track,
and at the tenth, I begin to curse
and not to myself. Meanwhile the nurse,
continuing work without a pause,
reserves her comments until she's through:
'This wasn't so bad. It hardly hurt.
You need a positive attitude.'
Then leaves me listening to her skirt

rustle down the antiseptic hall.
I'm free to go. I gather my things,
coat and hat and a lampshade I brought
for a friend even sicker than I
who can't get out and lives nearby.
But on the street when I feel the sting
of the wind pushing me to the wall,
I allow myself the chance to cry,

this once to luxuriate in pain,
to bathe myself in the swirling tide
of the purest grief and then to ride
out agony so that I can reach
what has always stood on the other side:
a hopelessness that is not despair,
but a truth meant to bring me no where
except to myself and to this time.

And there I am in the busy street
surrounded by those who do not care
whether I'm to live, or how, or where
as long as I ask nothing of them.
They turn as I stagger on my feet,
a joke that can't even force a groan,
a drunken reveler who stands alone,
his humorless lampshade in his hand.

If now it seems I have only pain
to remind me that my life is real,
I mention it not as an appeal
for sympathy or understanding,
rather from a wish to make it plain
that it's earned a certain tender love
that I used to give to other things
which now I have no desire of."

He smiled at me—the lesson done.
and grabbed the tab and rose from his seat,
"Next time," he said, "it'll be your treat,
that is if there'll be another one."
He took from the rack his coat and hat,
a half-read book and a hand-carved cane,
and throwing a kiss to where I sat,
walked out through the cool Manhattan rain.

Easter Sunday, 1991

A Dream of Nightingales

in memory of Jerry Thompson

The Friday before your funeral I taught
Keats to my sophomore class. Little did they care
for the truth of beauty or the grace of truth,
but his being "half in love with easeful death"
penetrated through the smugness of their youth,
and I thought of you drawing me to the rear
window one early spring to hear in rapture
a bird hidden among the flowering pear.

You held your cat tight so that he could not scare
off such music as hadn't been heard all winter.
When you flew South to escape the arctic blast
and home again heard that dark-winged creature sing,
tell me, did he then reveal himself at last
as you believed he'd be—pure and beckoning?

A Part for Horn

I don't recall his name, but his death
made all the papers. In the school yard
we passed around forbidden copies
of the *Daily News* with photographs—
that back alley where he was found,
the outline of his naked body
barely visible beneath the sheet.

For a moment even the fat girls
with smudged blue eye shadow stopped giggling,
and the black kids, who leapt like dolphins
beneath the basketball hoops, hung fire;
Latinos, who reigned by divine right
in the handball courts, instinctively
bowed their heads and crossed their hard torsos.

Since he was new at school, he was made
a third trumpet in our concert band.
From my vantage in the sax section
I could observe his pale face darken
as he blew hard into the mouthpiece.
Once Mr. Vitalli ordered him to stand
alone and play the sad legato

of Mussorgsky's "Great Gate of Kiev"
which traditionally had begun
our spring program. Anxiously we watched
as his fingers trembled on the valves
and the flat notes sputtered and cracked. But
with the piece done, he bowed so gravely
that the whole class burst into applause.

Even Mr. Vitalli, whose aim
had been to humiliate him, saw
that here was a student whose inborn
sense of the absurd placed him beyond
the restraints of shame and honor
or other cheap pedagogic tricks
with which our teachers were familiar.

But also it freed him from the need
for admiration. The perfect child,
lithe as a whippet, whose seal-slick thatch
of hair slung low across his eyelids,
was indifferent to all about him
though ready to carry on his back
the world's weight or the heavier void.

I wish I could give you a picture
of him as he sat alone, later, waiting
for Mr. Vitalli's cue and not
the grade school graduation photo
published in the *Times* with hair combed back,
an unfocused smile blurring his face,
two passionless and babyish eyes.

I wish a camera had been there
to catch him as I saw him: a Jew
whose skin was as luminous and pure
as a page of the Torah before
the flame-like letters scorch across it,
with lips made sensuous and firm
by a faith in unfulfilled desire.

None of us knew what homeroom he had,
though surely one with the slowest boys
from which he'd rise to attend Music.
A friend once had him in gym where he
always emerged last from the shower
as though he had lost his way in the steam.
At lunch he disappeared completely.

He never ate, though once I saw him
in the darkest corner of the yard,
wrapped in an old herringbone topcoat
that hung down to his feet. There pigeons
devotedly pecked bits of sandwich
until a gust of wind blew open
his coat, and he took wing like a god.

Later the homicide detective
spoke of the need for information
and left behind a number to call
if we could remember any clues:
a name he might have mentioned, a stray
remark he might have made,
a stranger who might have met him at the gate.

But it was useless for him to ask.
We had reached that age when all our loves
were secrets kept even from ourselves
whose desires of unspeakable
proportions were held in bounds by fear
and ignorance of what might bring them
abatement if not satisfaction.

Nor could we explain how one of us
had courage enough to leave his home
for the embrace of men lured to bars,
the uncertainty of their kindness,
the unfamiliar, unmade beds, which
having filled the momentary need,
are left the morning after vacant.

Nor could I admit the guilt I felt
was a kind of vanity, for what
I wanted to confess to him would
not have changed his fate. Had I told him
how I dreamt at night of his fingers
playing upon me, pressing my skin
like the ivory keys of his trumpet,

his cheeks flushed from the sound that rose up
from my throat—he still would have run off
into the inconsolable night
to give his body to thankless men
and fall through the cracks of the city,
and still the papers would drop his tale
and leave the murder as yet unsolved.

Though twenty years have passed, I often
will think of him when I find myself
afraid with a stranger beside me,
when I watch children in the school yard
playing, or when, as tonight, I hear
faintly from a distance, a student
up in his room practicing the horn.

II

In the Summer Crucible

I have watched the grubs at night
crawling halfway up a tree
then burst open from the back
with another ghostly self,
pale as moonlight in moonlight,
their wings damp and glistening.

The next day the empty cells
cling still to the bark; while high
up in the branches, cicadas
fan flickering leaves with black,
dry wings and hiss like a pot
ready to boil over.

Planting the Garden

Admittedly I've made a mess of it—
too hasty as always from the get-go,
mulching, as you say, where angels fear to spread.
But really, John, I didn't intend to start
a garden—I just wanted some small dash
of color on the dried stubble of grass
the owner who sold us the place called *lawn;*
close-cropped and bald in spots, it looked much more
like the top of a middle-aged marine
than what others would call *vegetation.*

What harm could it do? one stroke of purple,
white or mauve in the blank expanse of weed?
And simple enough with a nursery
but five feet away from the hardware store,
that second home of all new home-buyers.
I glance over the sad display they've set
on the sidewalk, tables covered with trays
of asters, mums and packets of seed,
the old-maid's lace of unsold Dusty Miller.
I grab a couple of each on the run,
afraid of just what I cannot answer

but when I get home I practically fling
them at the earth like a dark imprecation,
the curse that I must sow and sow again.
"What have you done?" you ask, "You need to think
these things out: where best to put the beds,
and then what's best to put in them, prepare
the soil that they will have the right conditions."
But it's too late. The garden has begun.
I'm wedded to only one imperative:
Plant as much as you can before the winter comes.

A Jew, brought up in the city, what could
I learn of botany or horticulture?
Your mother's hands were all green thumbs, and you
followed in her vegetable love. What now?
I read with relish what I should have done.
But what I've always known is from Day One
the Garden has been a place for Error,
most of which finds its way to forgiveness.
I'm destined to make a harvest of it,
a priceless bouquet of misdemeanor.

That's why I bridle at your suggestion
that we hire a landscape architect
to draw up a master plan. "Do you know
enough to do it right?" you ask as though
it's Pride that prods me, when all along
it's fear that there might come an early end
to all this joyous confusion that's made
me resist the expert's advice. I beg:
Just give me more time to make mistakes,
grant me the grace that comes from doing wrong.

The Fury of Flowers

What has made the rose so angry
that for weeks, it has raised its ivory buds
like white-knuckled fists railing at the sky?

Was it something I did, or left undone?
Too little water? Not enough peat?
An unflattering light in the back garden?

Only when it opens do I see
the source of its discontent,
not civilization, but bees

drawn by its tea-brewed scent
rudely prying apart the petals one
by one until they get what they want.

At night the white rose glows like the moon
wearied with rage, alone and cold,
and it is only June.

Mockingbird Moderne

Once out of nature I shall never take
My bodily form from any natural thing . . .

—*W. B. Yeats*

Each morning I awaken
to a mockingbird who's taken
its song from a car alarm—
not the ones that beep
for fifteen minutes then sleep,
but the newer kind that keep
changing their tune of violation,
the whoop, whoop, whoop,
turning on a dime
into ratchet-a-ratchet-a-ratchet,
before going into a round
of Schoenberg cuisinarted—
wolf howls
sliced and ground
puréed with the curdled sound
of a half-hearted
exercise in French long vowels
ee-oh-ee-oh-ee-oh.
And just as I think he's done
he starts where he'd begun
as a thousand shrill boy choirs.
He'd drive the drowsy emperor in Yeats
to tempt those old malicious fates
and rip out all his wires.

Bonzai for Beginners

What
the West
would achieve
by leverage, the East
would produce through scale. "Give me a
point and I will move the world," declared Archimedes.

"Make
it small
enough," said
the Zen master who
held a pebble in his hand
and fingered the continents encrusted on its shell.

Trees
that we
can only see piecemeal because
of their size can be studied whole
when reduced to the dimensions of a common bread box.

Such
wisdom
lies behind
the bonzai whose large
appeal appears undiminished
in those who feel the power of its concentration.

Here
I stand
with a pine
seedling John brought back
from the beach for me, its green quills
like eyeless darning needles jabbed into a cushion.

Shall
I cut
its taproot
and plant it in some
pot no bigger than a thimble
as Mr. Morati directs in his manual?

Wrap
around
its limp trunk
and stubby branches
a bright armature of wire
so that it gleams like a maloccluded twelve year old

sent
against
his will to
the orthodontist?
Condemn it to a life of forced
confinement like the foot of a Mandarin princess?

All
beauty
is a form
of perversity,
the strange mutation
of chromosome and circumstance
than can make either a monster or a masterpiece.

But
the role
I play in
nurturing such freaks
is not beyond my frail control.
The oddities of nature may be nipped in the bud

should
I care
to nip them,
not letting my plots
be overgrown with anything
but the usual assortment of household flora.

Here
in the
U. S. A.
we have no need to
shrink the life around us and drive
it inward, introjecting its vital outward thrust

Why
stifle
what is great
within us? Such arts
have no part in modernity
and are better suited for the medieval zeitgeist

where
the whole
may be viewed
in one sitting and
inferred from any of its parts,
its locks opened by the same golden synecdoche,

where
Christ may
be revealed
in three dimensions,
his passion scene expertly carved
in a rosary no bigger than a horse chestnut.

I
want to
be weaned from
this old illusion
of completeness that brought heaven
and earth into the same compass as a grain of sand,

rid
myself
from the need
of totality
and draw my comfort from what won't
add up or by omission round to a graceful close.

Goya's Enlightenment

We surround him, this poor man from Asia
whom Goya left squatting in the center
   of an otherwise blank leaf,

and in the lowered lighting of the room
(dimmed to keep the pencil marks from fading)
   I read what's left of his face:

innocent? madman? clown? or imbecile?
a Katzenjammer Kid in karate
   robes? a moonchild in eclipse?

He has set his hair on fire until
he gets something—just what doesn't matter—
   anything, we're told, will do.

So great is his poverty that he's got
only his locks to lose, and by them gain
   his small share of attention.

But I give him only the briefest look—
so much to see—and turn my head aside
   hoping he won't realize

I'm afraid to make the decisive move
of breaking the glass and crossing the page
   and dousing his flaming thatch

of hair. I step back scorched and stumble through
more galleries, a bald-headed beggar
   without so much as a match.

Pictures at an Eakins Exhibition

The pains which Eakins has taken with his paints
are mirrored in the faces of his models:
the nurse in the Agnew Clinic, for instance,
bears what no male in the limelight bears, the pain
of the patient's incision, for the trials
of witnessing are reason enough to wince.

Yet still she stares, unlike the draped figure bent
in the Gross Clinic's corner who tries to shield
her face in the sleeve of coal-black bombazine
and claw at the shaft of light which has revealed
her child's body opened to the sight of men
and to their hard and glittering instrument.

Or Max Schmitt in his single scull who now whirls
back to face the painter, squints because the sun
on the Schuylkill burns his eyes. Even at peace
he feels the ache in America, lets hang
his thick arms as bare and useless as a girl's
and waits patiently the evening's dark release.

Two Muses

1. Mozart's Canary

Purchased in the market for a song
because I sang so brightly he forgot
how dull my plumage was: the green mixed brown
and gray, the yellow paling at my throat.

He hung me in the window while the sun
drove me mad with thoughts of home, then took
my songs—desperate with joy and resignation—
took them down with a rapid, workman's stroke.

Listen to *The Magic Flute*. Tamina—
me. Poppigano—me. The Queen
of the Night—yes, even she. All singing what
I poured into his ear: *free me, free me.*

He said he'd let me go when he had filled
his next commission, but then the requiem
arrived, and then. . . . I watched him fevered and chilled,
and with the fleeting light claimed my revenge:

I just refused to change my tune to sorrow;
each sound I made was insolent with life.
In the end he begged to have me carried off
to this back room where I have spent all winter

tilting my head up to the tainted mirror.
I watched my thin, white crown of feathers molt
like a powdered wig, then spill half notes like seeds
against the bars grown colder than the dead.

2. Mapplethorpe's Lily

It waited—which is what flowers do best,
waited for him to tire of men who bent
and bled and bound themselves beneath the blank
stare of the camera's lens, waited until
their pliant skin hardened into Tuscan
stone, until exhausted with the effort
of exposing in the human form what
was perfect in it all along, he turned

as others had before him and found
in the lily's frail permanence of flesh,
what he'd been missing: then and only then
did it open fully and let him in
to a satisfaction that needed no
desire, a death without embarrassment.

A World of Difference

We put her off as long as we could with claims
of rotting floorboards, toilets that would not flush,
and other excuses, all equally lame.

But now in the vestibule she stands in wait
to see whether we've achieved to her account
the minimal standards of civilized life.

The last time this former neighbor visited
we had just taken title to our new home,
a hundred-year-old Italianate townhouse.

She reviewed the rooms as if they were ruins
out of the mezzotints of Hubert Robert,
the ones where gypsies camp on the grounds sacred

to a minor goddess, where fresh-hung laundry
billows in the viaduct's fallen arches
and a lone girl dances the tarantella.

In my neighbor's wake half-pints of Ripple ebbed,
peeling sheets of wallpaper stuck out their tongues
as if to say, "Ahh," and the unhinged doors flew

open to expose their crazed interiors.
Up in the attic she found the burnished spoons
of junkies and dogs' excremental remains.

"Frankly," she concluded, "I can't imagine
how even Herculean efforts could bring
this building back to life. Some dead are beyond

our superhuman powers of resurrection
and should be razed for their own good. Take this old
widow's advice: cut your losses—get out now."

We didn't, of course. And after three years' labor
she's back, running her gloved hand across the scraped
and newly repainted lusterboard wainscot

whose pattern of intertwining rose stems forms
an intricate quasi–art nouveau design.
She fingers vases, a box of silver, checks

the hallmarks on a set of porcelain plates,
remarks the retouched scaglioli mantle
which replaced a smashed one of Georgian marble.

Finally returning to that upper floor
where the dogs and the drug addicts roamed, painted
now innocent shades of green and lined with books,

she faces us to report at last, "You boys
have made a world of difference! Can this be
the same place?" We stand at the dormer window

and watch the skyline looming in the distance
The latticework of unfinished offices
graph the starry rise of corporate structures.

From the street below float up the clump and jingle
of an aging pony hauling his cart full
of primary-colored fruits and vegetables

and the radio blare of a box the size
of a child's coffin borne on the shoulder
of a teenage boy. Two girls in choir robes

rush by laughing on their way to a service,
and the ancient black man who runs the car wash
hums loudly his ancient, sanctifying hymn.

I am humbled by all these fallen creatures
of the world who've taught me that even harder
than the act of making is the act of re–

making and, as Yeats said, "those that build . . . again
are gay." I want to tell my former neighbor
that no one can *make* a world of difference;

at best we uncover what's already there
so various and true, beyond our meager
powers to recognize or to comprehend.

Now I feel the beauty of my transgressions
against the entropy and dissolution
which also is a part of my inheritance.

As the angel locked the gates to Paradise
and the road lay all before them in the dusk,
Eve might have felt this thing and said to Adam:

"Look, love, we have made a world of difference,"
thereby showing her mate how all creative
acts begin as civil disobedience.

And looking from my perch, I see the garden
of the nursing home across the street where folk
in gleaming wheelchairs circle round a fountain

in which from waves unwavering in support
forever leaps a dolphin, upon whose back
we take a slippery hold and dream of rest.

III

The Path of Least Resistance

On our first night in Paris,
exhausted from the crossing,
we are lost on the Rive Gauche,
in rues I rued we traveled.
2 A.M., light drizzle and
no one to ask directions.

"If we can get to the Seine,
I can find our way," I said.
But how to find the river?
Hard now, the rain soaked my shoes.
Then it struck me: *go downhill.*
And it was downhill from there.

The Great Trans-Atlantic
Hot-Air Balloon Race

At nine a Danish frigate spotted them
and apprised the authorities on shore.
By midday the bluffs were teaming. Ladies
lounged from the backs of open limousines

and the mayors from five neighboring townships
fought over the honor of conferring
medallions on the winners. Boys traveled
the coast on their bicycles bringing back

unreliable reports of sightings.
Such wonder was part of the lethargy
of August when even the monstrous
birth of a piglet or calf occasions

the general interest and amusement.
Crowds moved up and down the shore, raising wet
fingers to prevailing winds. Bonfires
flared up at regular intervals.

An accordion's wheezing could be heard
over children splashing in the shallows.
Lovers strolled through the migratory dunes
out of reach of their suspicious parents.

At dusk with fruits plucked from picnic hampers,
the postman juggled persimmon and plum
till he lost them in the wine-colored sky
where they hid among the constellations.

Weeks went by. Rumors floated. Some men claimed
it had been a hoax. Then the weather chilled.
People were forced to attend to business,
and at last the harvest was carried in.

The North Country

for Diana and Sandi

1. Along Hadrian's Wall

Every empire learns its limits, and here
the Romans called theirs to a halt, sealing
their border with a row of piled stones
as greasy and gray in the steady rain
as so many balls of wax. I wonder
how the wall sticks to the ground which has grown
so slippery even the cows have lost
their footing in the steep and glassy fells.

This morning in hopes of beating the rain
we rose just before dawn and headed straight
to Mithra's Temple where the winter solstice
is marked, some say, by the sun's appearance
in the cleft of its eastern wall. We found
on our arrival the ruins flooded
and all his retinue of Persian slaves
kneeling in an inch or two of water.

Yet once Mithra had chased the local gods
away and claimed this country as his own,
unless they gladly washed their hands of it—
a treeless waste where only aliens
feel at home and even the rocks erupt
into foreign forms, like this crag whose face,
as though set on an Easter Island shore,
stares down upon the clouds of mindless sheep.

At dusk—which falls at four—we take our tea
at an abbey where the white-cowled monks
long ago gave way to girls in well-starched
uniforms. We poke the fire. It is far
too late by now to make it back by light.
We'll have to travel under the cover
of dark, and in the car, we watch night teethe
along the crusty edges of a star:

When the gods retire, this is what they leave.

2. Durham Cathedral

The Venerable Bede faces west
in the Galilee Chapel where he may catch
the late afternoon sun, pearl-like strung
across the throat of the River Wear.

And at the cathedral's eastern end
Saints Cuthbert and Oswald lie in a section
screened off behind the central altar.
Legend says that friends in life, they held

such passionate disdain for woman
a line was inscribed across the nave, beyond
which no female was ever to step—
even queens who dared to sleep the night

in the church's grounds were forced to seek
more distant shelter for fear their saintly wrath
would crack the rafters and send flying
buttresses into a headlong dive.

Since then their anger has abated.
I watch one old lady kneel and touch their tomb
without a trace of trepidation.
Still, men seem most at ease here.

Priests sail by us, their robes like black jibs
catching the light, celestial breezes; their stiff
clothes rustle and whisper like lovers
who have stayed awake the whole night through.

Beside me a statue of the saints
depicts Cuthbert holding the head of Oswald,
though his own has long been missing, hacked
off, I think, in the time of Cromwell.

Yet one head is enough to reveal
the miracle: art grows old, but the body
of the saint suffers no corruption.
What worm dare turn in his sacred flesh?

This is no Medusa, horrible
to behold, a scalp oozing with foul vipers,
but a face that calmly looks beyond
the world, clasped, not at arm's length, but as

a mother might clutch her child when she
fears it may be stolen away—and he had
every reason to be afraid. Who
knew into whose hands their bones might fall?

How many years did it take before
their brothers could find a place for them to lie
in safety—they who'd done nothing worse
than love words and men in that order?

3. A House of Two Women

In this house of two women, two
women, that is, and their two cats,
I feel I am a welcomed guest,
but not for a second at home.
Why should I be? The gift I came
two thousand miles to find is not
the comfort of the familiar.
Not that I'm uncomfortable.
All day as though drunk on clouds
the light has staggered through the room.
The persian purrs across my knees.
Yet even these pleasures remind
me sharply that I'm on foreign ground.

In this house of two women, there
is nothing on display. The rooms,
packed with living, unfold themselves
only to the gentlest touch.
When I inquire about a piece—
a torso carved in bas-relief
on wood dredged from the riverbed,
part of a hull sunk long ago—
they pass me the figure to feel
her shoulders, hips and breasts ground smooth
by the current, and stroke the form
since hand cannot trust eye to see.

They devote each room to a task
or tasks: this table's where they sew,
and here the dinners are assembled

(from local rabbits, apples, greens),
here a book is being written,
and there a letter to a friend.
The windowsills alone are free
of all encumbrances to let
the cats attend to leaves and cars
and fretful grackles in the yard
for this, I'm told, is the cats' home too.

And in this house of two women,
I am reminded by the mass
of my body, my heavy tread,
and the dark timbre of my voice
that I'm, beyond all else, a man.
In the white mirror of the tub,
I watch my shaggy arms and legs
cast their coarse hairs to the waters,
and carefully I comb the soap
to rub away whatever lean
inscription I might leave behind,
and when I step out of my bath
and knock the pumice from the rim,
cracking its tip on the floor, I feel
rebuked by my ungainliness
that cannot help but violate
the smoothness of this fluid world.

So on my departure when you turned
to say "No one who's stayed has left
so little sign of being here"
I felt proud and a bit ashamed,

for even this poem, I'm afraid,
may be no more than silence
vandalized by song. Enough
that you had let me in and said
that I might come again to this,
your house, and your two gracious cats.

Thanksgiving in Bucks Country

in memory of Bernard Barrow

Shyly they come to the edge of the pond
to eat the corn my host has left and lap
the salt lick smoother than a frozen lake.
All morning we have heard the deadly clap—
rifles discharging periodic rounds.

I cannot help but feel the deer have come
for our protection, half aware in some
animal way that they are safe as long
as they keep near the house, yet just as strong
must be the fear that drives them to approach.

We watch their rouged flanks rustle in the breeze
like stiff silk gowns. And for a while it's we
who are held captive by desire and fear,
reluctant to disturb them at their ease.
But at last a door opens, and they flee

to the uncertain shelter of the wood,
unwilling to trust us any further.
That afternoon I find near where they stood,
a pile of buckshot one had left behind,
unloaded into the short, brittle grass.

Tom's Cove, Assateague

From the car window, we're allowed to watch
the ghostly ponies graze in the moonlight,
munching the grass at the roadside stop.
The signs posted everywhere remind us:
DO NOT FEED THE ANIMALS. KEEP THEM WILD.

But a black one, star-struck between her eyes,
flips back her mane like a schoolgirl, upset
that we won't roll our window down and hand
over the stale pretzel she's been eyeing
in the corner of the dash. She's not fooled.

There is no place more civilized than this:
the deer come within arm's length, quite certain
they've nothing to fear, and even the plump
and pampered flies sting with a certain smugness
as if they, too, were a protected species.

How much care has gone into preserving
this aura of untouchablity:
egrets, as white and stiff as ballboys
on a tennis court, array themselves across
the manicured salt marshes, and the dunes,

which if unattended would wander off
like idiot children or the drooling mad,
are tacked down by long tufts of pubic grass,
which we are warned (more signs again)
not to walk upon or lie among nude.

I watch from this umbilical spit of sand,
as clouds form over Tom's Cove, form and fade
when they cross low over warmer ground,
then reform when blown further out to sea.
Look, that one's a Spanish galleon circling

the harbor. There's a sword, and this one's rolled
up like a hedgehog. These at least remain
on the loose as they've always been, renewed
without our cultivation. They and the thick
American light, diffuse and indifferent,

allowing no shadows and no secrets.
The fry spawn in its steady gaze and then
are eaten, and on the shallow island
to the south, NASA's savage ears are turned
to the crackle of dry and withered stars.

Crazy Woman Falls, Wyoming

It was the child who saw it first,
the ten year old, a few steps from his mother
who held the hand of his younger brother;
It raised its head and gave its tail a shutter
as if it were about to burst.

She gasped and held her son close to her side.
We all stopped then, uncertain and afraid
and watched the knotted hank of Indian braid
assess if we intended to invade
this bank where snakes reside.

A second more of waiting, and then he slid
sidelong through the thick and glossy green:
undulant, unhurried, and a bit obscene,
something the children should not have seen,
a grown-up's secret best kept hid.

But once in camp we're forced to confide
to the men who brought us just what we've met.
"You stay right here. We'll get him yet."
And sure enough in an hour they've set
the rattler free from his scaly hide,

which is left to air in the flat of a truck
while they open their beers and start to play
a round of poker that will last all day.
At dusk they pack and drive us away,
grumbling and giddy about their luck.

IV

While Sodom Was Occupied

While Sodom was occupied
with strange guests visiting Lot,
two youths escaped through the gates
into the encircling plains
where alone all night they lay
under the indulgent stars.

At dawn on the road away
from the burning city, they
passed first a pillar of salt
in the shape of a woman
and then a man weeping tears
none of his children could stop.

The Guide of Tiresias

I think of Oedipus, old, led by a boy
—*Thom Gunn*

Never was there a time when I did not lead him,
when I did not feel his hand upon my shoulder.

Never was there a time I was not his eyes
to tell him here lies Thebes, and there stands Corinth,

here the rocks have given way, and there two snakes coil
like twisted rope looking for a neck to hang on.

Sometimes I thought he was my mother, so gently
did he hold me when I was sick, so tenderly

did he wash me at the end of a long journey,
when he could barely stand, his arms stiff and shriveled.

Sometimes I thought he might be my father, so strong
was his grip on my body to keep me from danger,

so firm his warnings, so stern his admonitions,
And then at times he was my child, and hungrily

fed on my warmth and caresses, afraid of what
others—burning with questions—might force him to say.

"What will happen to us?" he would cry at nightfall
as if he did not already know the answer.

Second Sight

for Eileen Gregory

I knew before it came that the call
was coming, but this wasn't one I wanted
to answer. On the other end was Gil
pleading: "The leads are cold, Amanda.
The trails go nowhere. I'm stuck." What could I say?
Gil's a good man and I've worked with him before.
"Just bring me some clothes the kid would wear,
Pj's if you can, a pullover sweater,
a toy he liked to play with and a blanket."

For weeks the Allen boy's been missing.
The mother told police she saw a stranger
lurking in the neighborhood, a drifter-type,
a black man in his middle twenties
but no one else has seen him. On the TV
she's begged for her son's return, her husband
close beside her, though he seemed unable
to move, his eyes fixed and dim like two headlights
left on all day without the motor running.

In an hour I heard Gil's squad car
crunch gravel. Crystal, my daughter, let him in
and took the satchel, then laid the contents out
across the kitchen table. "The kid
didn't wear pajamas, but he slept in these."
Gil pointed to a Power Ranger T-shirt.
I touched it and knew in a second
the boy was dead. "We figured as much" was all
Gil said. I felt for more. "He's not gone far.

The body's very close to his home."
"How close?" Gil asks. "I won't be able to tell
until I get there." That's when my Crystal says,
"I want to come, too." I looked at Gil
who nodded, but I hung back. I've suspected
awhile that Crystal takes after her mother
in having what they call *second sight.*
She hasn't said anything, but I can see
how she drifts away while eating her dinner

or even fighting with her brother—
not that silly daydream look teenage girls get
(she has that, too) but something more disturbing:
as if she knows what's next to happen,
tuned in, let's say, between two distant channels,
one picture superimposed on the other.
I can't explain what happens. It's like
trying to remember a name you once knew,
perhaps the first wife of a distant cousin.

First you're blank, then everything rushes
forward—you see the mole beside her lips, hear
her laughter and the solemn words she's made up
to impress the preacher, and you can't
even keep yourself from smelling the perfume
she's bought on sale down at the local K-Mart.
I was her age when it became plain
I had the gift. Some gift! An obligation,
you shouldn't have to pay and yet keep paying,

as if your life were charged on plastic
and you could never get beyond the interest.
I'm her mother and, sure, I know there's nothing
I can do to stop her from herself,
and yet I want to say: *Keep your eyes shut tight.*

You don't have to accept what the gods offer.
It was quiet in the car as Gil
reported our ETA. Crystal cradled
a dumptruck and kept spinning its plastic tires.

I rubbed my cheek against the collar
of the boy's frayed baseball jacket. That's when it
came to me, this scene—a stream with a bridgehead,
and a bank of slippery sumac.
It's night and the hard stars outline the tree tops.
"Connect the dots," I say aloud and Crystal
stiffens—she too has seen a pattern.
"There's a nest right above his head," she whispers,
and I'm afraid because I've sensed birds sleeping.

When we get to the Allen home, there's
the father on the front porch while his wife
is on the lawn, screaming: "Get that woman out
of here, so help me, I'll sue you blind.
She'll turn this thing into a three-ring circus!"
"I'm sorry. She must have heard me radio
ahead," Gil says, but I don't pay him
any mind 'cause Crystal's running for the woods
behind the Allens' as if she knows just where

she's headed. "He's somewhere just above
this ridge," she confides in me when I catch up.
Gil and another policeman follow close,
but Mrs. Allen is far behind.
It's spring and already the earth is covered
with dense foliage. Brambles snag our ankles,
catch the edges of our jeans, and mud
is smeared around our Nikes. I hug
again the Power Ranger T-shirt, then hear

water rustling in a stony creek
like a sleeper twisted in his fresh starched sheets.
I reach for Crystal and try to hold her back.
But she shouts, "It's not too much further."
I hurt. Then a robin, blood upon his breast,
comes swooping with a thread of worm in his beak
heading straight for a holly, whose hard
and shiny leaves are like a thousand shields raised
for protection. She bends to see what's beneath

the limbs. I pull her back more roughly
than I intend. She turns and shrieks, "Mama,
Mama, why do you want to hurt me?" But it's
not to me she speaks, but Mrs. Allen
gasping at our side, who hears once more her son
before she silenced him. I hear the gurgle
in his throat, and hold my baby tight.
Then with blinding sight we both become aware
we will never feel my love so clear again.

Field Notes

for Carolyn Bocian

For the first three months I took no notes.
One look at me, and they'd set off so quickly
even my guides, the best in all the jungle,
soon fell behind. It took half a year
of staring high into the upper mantle
to learn the difference between the wind's light pulse
and my monkeys passing overhead.

They posed unusual problems for research:
each week my band would meet up with another
family group of the same species,
and together forage for a day or two,
sharing the rough task of caring for the young,
and keeping alert for predators.
But then suddenly the groups would move apart.
Which one was I to follow? Which pack was mine?
The easiest way of keeping track
is to select the most distinctive member,
one so deformed by accident or warfare,
that he stands as marker for the rest.
In my case this method did not work. My band
was perfect—each and every one a flawless
specimen, distinguished if at all
by age, weight, sex or size. I would have given
anything for just one mutation, some freak
of nature with belly striped with gold,
a cork-screwed tail, a benign deformity
I could clearly make out from the ground below.

They liked to toy with me by hiding
whenever I approached. It started from fear,
but then became a game, which I lost, of course.
Once they disappeared for ten whole days.
I worried like a mother. I sent my men
to blanket their territory, splitting up
the feeding grounds into small sectors.
Still no luck. At last, I knew they'd have to come
to me. I sent all the carriers away,
sat beneath a tree they visited,
smoked half a pack of Camels and fell asleep.
When I awoke they were looking down at me,
the tufts of their cheeks, a frizzy puff,
like enormous dandelions going to seed.
They clucked together, amused and pitying,
the younger ones squealing with laughter.

When I first came they scrawled across the green leaves
of the Tembu trees like faint lines of drying
invisible ink, a text that soon
could only be read when the full sun had burnt
it through. But at the end—the last four months—
they were as clear as my diary,
whose delicate shorthand needs only transcription
before it can be read. They were like banners
spread over the beach in summertime,
dragged low from the tail of a toylike biplane,
a fleeting message punctuated by shrieks
and rustling, telling you where to eat
and how best to protect yourself from dangers.

The men I've dated since returning stateside
have been as confused by my actions
as I was at first by my troop of monkeys,
unable to understand my simplest gestures.
In bed they're puzzled by my response.
I feel I should explain, "This sigh means pleasure;
this one is boredom, and this last is a sign
of resignation." I'm a foreign
film that lost its subtitles, a capsized signal
floating on the airwaves. I am waiting for one,
just one man to watch me half as long
as I watched my band of monkeys, a man who
thinks I'm worthy of even that attention.
But none so far has felt compelled
to try to decode my meaning. All their lives
they've been taught to feel their existence alone
was gift enough. Were I to swing arm
over arm across the ceiling and then hang
from the chandelier, how long would they remain
contented merely to sit beneath?

The little ones neared me first. They were braver,
and hardly knew a time when I wasn't there
collecting my data beneath them.
I pretended not to notice their approach,
busying myself with notebooks or samplings.
The males to show how fearless they were
crept to the ground and crouched beside a Yako

lost in the filigree of fronds and tassels.
By offering food, I knew I could
make them bolder, but I couldn't encourage them.
Mine was a study of their life in the wild
and relies on maintaining the fine
distinction between tolerance and friendship.
What I had to become was just a presence
that would neither frighten nor alter
their behavior so they would go on as though
I was not there. Don't think it didn't hurt,
my effort to be nothing to them.
I have never seen creatures more beautiful,
but theirs was a beauty I could never touch,
no matter how much I wanted to.
I'd dream of stroking my fingers through their soft
tufted fur, of lying among them, balled up
asleep in the crook of a tall tree
like some strange fruit unfit for plucking. I dreamed
of waking at first light with their tails like vines
wrapped around me, their mouths at my breast.

Once a mature female lost her grip and plummeted
to the earth. I couldn't tell if she were dead
or merely knocked unconscious. I wanted
to lift her up and carry her back to camp
where she could be treated. But I did not dare.
Finally she stirred and staggered up
the tree screeching—her leg probably broken.
For a time it was hard for her to keep up
with the others, so one juvenile
male—perhaps her son—was assigned to assist
and the band perceptibly slowed its travels,
though it never stopped circulating

through the forest. It was then, in fact, I got
my finest data. I was sorry when she
at last had recovered well enough
to fade once more into the high foliage,
screened out from my unsought, intruding glances.

O those blessed wounds that brought love near!
How they allowed me access to the untouched
beauty of their lives! How odd it is that pain
should be the threshold from which we may
express what we may never put our hands on.
Three years I watched them while they regarded me
with neither dislike nor suspicion.
I see them still as they rested at midday
grooming each other with immaculate care.
They must have known—don't you think?—that my
attention was love of a similar kind
that asks nothing but the privilege to keep watch
over their far and perfect bodies.

The Witness to the Arrest

Mark 14:50–52

It is what each of us hopes will happen
should soldiers come to carry us away,
the dinner guests flown with the fatal kiss,
the servants scrambling through the kitchen door,

that a youth will follow from behind
alone in his linen shirt, having rushed
from his slim bed to witness our going,
that he will keep a distance safe enough

so when guards turn at last to arrest him
they will grab only the hem of his gown,
which, giving way, will allow him naked
to flee through the darkness by which he came.

From then on, we will see before us, not
the betrayal of the many we loved,
nor the indifference of those we served, but
the slow shock of his escaping beauty.

The Psalm of Prometheus

*Throughout the happy Golden Age, only men
were upon the earth; there were no women.
Zeus created these later, in his anger at
Prometheus for caring so much for men . . .*

—Edith Hamilton

What do gods eat? he asked,
although he wasn't hungry.

They eat the tender edges of your ears, I answered,
the bloody rosettes of your nipples.

He scowled. I am tired of fruit and crushed oats,
gnarled roots and the juice of ripened berries.

So I brought him the meats he wanted,
the pale loins of calves,

the shanks of mothering ewes,
birds plucked and gutted from the sky,

and he let me lick the back of his neck
and chew the space between his shoulder blades.

How do the gods eat this? he asked me, spitting out the raw
flesh, which was tough and stringy and impossible to chew.

We warm it first in the heat of our desire, I answered,
we seer it in the flames of passion.

I'm sick of cold mutton, he shouted,
throwing aside his helpings of uncooked goat and venison.

So I brought him fire,
which crackled like trampled twigs and hissed like startled cobra.

Only then did he let me feast on his body
until we both were sated.

Zeus, master of revenge,
no torture you'd have fashioned

could have inflicted more exquisite pain
nor brought my spirit lower—

not the chains that bite my skin as once I teethed on his,
not the mountain to which I'm bound as once I held him fast,

not even the eagle who plucks my liver through the wounds
that cannot heal—no, none of these could bring

the torment of watching him flail each night
with that woman you created at his side,

her pudgy fingers fluttering with pleasure
above her tightly lidded box.

V

My Father Almost Ascending

They've grown used to him, as he
goes out each morning to stand
among the ibis and crane.
Barely looking his way, they
call to one another, and
dry their delicate, long wings

It is when my mother shouts
excitedly from the house,
"You'll frighten off the birds,"
that they storm up as one
whirlwind of white, threatening
to take my father with them.

A Father's Blessings

Now that he is nearly deaf, my father can't
get enough music. It wasn't always this way.
When sound first began to forsake him, skipping
out for hours at a time, leaving behind
no note to say where it had gone, just a buzz
that hovered about his ears before it stung,

he responded like a spurned lover, forbad
its name to be mentioned, canceled his tickets
to the symphony and then turned the tweeters
of his stereo to the wall. My brother
was given his big band records—thick, glossy
seventy-eights that slept in the raveled sleeves

of their original albums. And I, I
was told never to practice in his presence.
He, who had listened with pleasure as I played
upon the mangled rippling of the Moonlight
Sonata or ineptly deconstructed
the Bach Two-Part Inventions, now shut his ears

and took whatever measures would make them stop.
But worse was that he gave up singing. His voice
which had filled the house with ballads and jingles
and eased us to sleep with mournful spirituals
sung in the deep-throated mode of Paul Robeson
was silenced, or rather, driven underground

to emerge like Philomel's complaint in flights
of rare, urgent song. But now at last the purge
is over. Each morning he sits listening
to the beasts broadcast their territorial
and erotic demands—furious herons
honking at the intruding swans, the loud plash

of mullets breaking open with muscled backs
the resisting surface of the slow canal.
At work in the garage, he whistles loudly
and at night he stares into the radio
as if he could watch the music escaping
into the living room—thin threads of music

like the pale hairs of light that appear to grow
from the luminous numbers on a dial.
When the melody rises above the range
of his reception to frequencies beyond
his grasp, he waits patiently for its return
and welcomes now the prodigal cadence home.

On my last visit, when unable to sleep,
I found my father reading my latest work.
"These I like," he said, "Were I a composer,
I'd set them to music," and then he sang
line after line, beating time with one hand free
and deaf to whatever his neighbors might say.

Daughters Denying the Dreams
of Their Father

Mother and her sisters tried to disabuse
their father of his dream—someday returning
to see the place where he was born, a village
so small no map has deigned to give it a dot.

Their objections were reasonable enough:
in his eighties, he was far too old to leave
on the long, harsh trip to Lithuania
should the Soviets issue him a visa.

Besides, if such a village still existed
(and with two world wars and a revolution
they had cause to doubt), it had probably changed
beyond human powers of recognition.

"Surely by now everyone you knew is dead,"
his daughters told him, "Even the boys with whom
you'd gone to school. Dead or moved away. Or else
they've long forgotten you and your family."

Against such arguments he was left no choice
but admit defeat. It was true what they said.
And he tried to freeze the animate faces
from his childhood into a final repose.

But they wouldn't rest, and for minutes or hours
or entire afternoons my grandfather,
with grandchildren tumbling loudly around him,
would be lost to us, lost in his reveries.

He was back among the invisible life of his youth,
leaping over the leaf-choked ruts
and hedges, smelling the barley fields at dusk
or the damp musk of pressed serge in the workroom.

In his ears were the cackles of old women
dickering over the price of gaberdine,
or the drone of flies as plump as ripe berries
and men arguing Talmud with the rabbis.

At ninety, he no longer spoke of going,
and his daughters rejoiced at their victory,
never expressing what they really dreaded,
the vision of the unchanged world of his birth:

houses blue and golden as a Marc Chagall
where girls open their arms to patchwork fiddlers.
A bridegroom's glass shatters into prickly stars,
and their father is lost to them forever.

The Gifts of Greece

The War crossed half of Europe off the list
of countries they could visit on the trip
Mom planned for Dad's seventy-fifth birthday.
He told her, "No places with memories,"
afraid that even after fifty years
some stray remark or minor incident—
a girl with baguette beneath her arm,
an empty bottle shattered in the street—
might trip the memory's long-stretched wire and bring
whizzing like shrapnel all the horror back.

So they went to Greece—no memories there,
except collective ones of archetypes
and architecture. They liked the light show
at the Parthenon best, then the ripple
of twilight on the Aegean, flashing
headlights of the taxis ricocheting
off the shell-shocked walls. Halfway to Delphi
my mother's knees gave out—a bad omen—
and at Ephesus, they wait for the strength
to return to their tattered ship and home.

At customs they have nothing to declare
except their gratitude for being back
and how little the dollar's worth these days.
The bored inspector waives them through with two
T-shirts, a tiny Trojan horse and this
clay mask of Dionysus which hangs here
eyeless on my wall, his long curls plaited
with grape and grape leaf, lotus and poppy,
the only thing they found that might amuse
their unaccountable, untraveled son.

Primal Scene

The day I am born
I play with my cousins
on the slope below
the hospital
where my mother
is lying-in.
It has snowed
the night before
and our hands sting
with the low voltage
of the cold.
Snowballs
one after another
graze her window,
and at last, my mother
looks out, raising
me up for everyone to see.
I have been told
this story so often
I no longer question
its truth, for no memory
is more vivid
than the ones we imagine.
There is my body
pink as a radish
and the black
tyrannical shock
of new fallen hair.

Heroic Measures

Angina pectoris being what it is,
my father is made to walk four miles a day
about the Floridian development
where he and my mother came to retire.

Down for my yearly visit, I go with him
on his rounds through the arching streets of stuccoed
single-story homes, spaced at equidistant
intervals and built to uniform standards.

All of the units sport canary yellow
carpeting and kitchens of laminated
avocado green. Every lawn is watered
on schedule, cut to regulation heights,

and where Ruskin hoped the Lamp of Memory
would blaze, I see the blank facades of total
amnesia, a whole community beset
by architectural Alzheimer's Syndrome.

My father frowns as we pass before a house
where a friend once lived, his comatose body,
interminably ill, lies like Tithonus
with those who've lost even the power to die.

"I don't want to be like him," my father says,
"strapped to a rack like a condemned heretic,
made to take food through the arm, my air piped in
like Musak from a hose taped to my gullet.

"Now while I'm healthy and my heart's in repair,
I want a promise: *No heroic measures*.
nothing to extend my life beyond its time,
to stretch it like an African women's throat

"bound to the chin with a noose of necklaces.
I don't want you or anyone to place me
in a state of suspended animation,
in the visionless sleep of the nearly dead."

He stopped, waiting for my oath: *No heroic
measures*. My hand raised in a Boy Scout salute.
Only then did he breathe a sigh of relief,
resume his normal rate of respiration.

Above us the dilated, subtropic sun
unchanging hung, and the palms fingered the calm
upper air. An egret posed by the stagnant
canal where thick fish slumbered on the bottom.

At our feet a cold-blooded lizard held stock
still, stonier than the stone on which it crouched,
frozen forever despite the steady heat
or the pulse that flickered below his green head.

Father, prisoner in this dull paradise,
come away with me North, where the seasons break
the undifferentiated days and leaves
fall from the chattering limbs of frozen elms,

where birds scuttle across the sky and huddle
in the ice-toothed eaves of variegated homes,
where children hear stories of their beginnings
and elders begin to see what is their end.